Bad Dad Good Dad

A real-life hellhole

Jim Clark

Published by

J. Charles Clark Publishing
a division of J. Charles Clark Consulting, Inc.
a member of the Clark Group of American Companies

All rights are the the property of

J. Charles Clark Consulting, L.P.

ISBN 978-0-578-17858-5

Printed in the United States of America

2nd Edition - 2022

Special Message

If you are living in a hell hole like the one described in this book, this book was written for you. Remember this, YOU ARE NOT ALONE.

The key to surviving a life in a hell hole is how you handle things. Don't let your circumstances get you down. Don't get depressed. Look to the future and the great life you will have someday. That day will come sooner than you think.

Work hard on your grades and earn a scholarship to college or trade school. Get an after-school job and earn some money. Buy yourself something nice. Buy your girlfriend something nice and take her out for a pizza.

Be careful with whom you associate. Do your own thing. Stay away from the drug dealers and other lowlifes. They'll take you down.

Don't give up. Be tough. Hang in there. You'll be out soon and free to build your own life. I KNOW what I'm talking about. I was the boy in this book. I lived in a real-life hell hole. I did exactly what I'm telling you to do and it worked. It worked for me and it will work for you.

God bless you my young friend. I'm thinking about you and praying for you. I'm looking forward to meeting you someday.

Your Uncle Jim

Special Dedication

This book is dedicated to Rosann and James Allen, who loved me and gave me a home away from home when I needed one the most.

High school isn't easy. When Rosann's daughter Kathy told Rosann she would not go out with me anymore because I didn't turn her on, Rosann told me straight up: "Son, you just don't turn her on. Dinner is at six". That was Rosann. Straight up, to the point, and full of love for anyone who needed it. James was her backup. Between the two, they spread God's love with their actions, with the way they lived.

"Son, you just don't turn her on. Dinner is at six," was the beginning of a lifelong friendship. Years later, I visited Mom Allen. As I was telling her about how we planned to feed every hungry child in America, she got up in the middle of my sentence and walked out of the room. When she came back, she had her checkbook. She said, "How do I make out the check?" NO hesitation. She didn't even bother to hear the whole story about how we planned to feed every hungry child in America. When she learned of an opportunity to help another human who was down, she moved into action. When I explained that we weren't taking donations, she told me to be sure to call her first if we ever did.

It's my prayer that every Little Jimmy who needs some love will find his Mom Allen and James. I thank God for helping me find mine.

Gender

This book is written for both boys and girls. To make the text less wordy and thereby the read easier, the male gender is addressed. The author trusts no offense will be taken.

Table of Contents

Prologue 13

Bad Dad 15

Good Dad 47

Two Ways Out 67

Good and Evil 69

Saved 73

Steps to Salvation 77

License to Sin 81

A Better Life Now 85

Epilogue 91

Epilogue II 95

Index 97

Prologue

I haven't used God's name in vain herein, nor have I used the f-word or any other hard-core profanity. I have, for the sake of realism, referred to light profanity with ---- marks. If you are profanity sensitive to the point that this will offend you, you should stop reading now. The book is as factual as 50 years of old memories will allow. While literary license is taken with some events, others have been left out completely because they are just too vile to mention. Overall, the text does a good job of describing the events that took place. Things happened pretty much as they are told.

It may sound like I'm just whining about my childhood, or trying to cast my dad and mom as the worst parents who ever lived. I am not. God gave me my parents, and He knows what He's doing. If I had it all to do over again, if I could choose my parents, I would choose Jim and Betty Clark, the parents that God gave me. The good that came from having them as parents far outweighs the bad.

"I'm coming, Jim!"

Bad Dad

When I was eleven, home was a dangerous environment. It was the middle of the night, and Dad had just punched mom in the face so hard that her false teeth came through her lower lip and were sticking out the front of her face like an elephant's tusk. My four younger brothers were cowered behind the couch, presumably because they were afraid for their own safety. So, I stepped in and protected Mom and them. Dad beat me almost to death. I knew little about fighting then, so I lowered my head and rammed him like a Billy goat. Not good. He grabbed me and lifted me off the ground and beat me on the table. I couldn't get loose. Every time I came down, my chest hit first. I don't remember how often he slammed me. All I remember is hearing him call me a little son-of-a-b----, and then, SLAM! SLAM again, and SLAM again, and SLAM again. It hurt, it hurt a lot. Finally, when I realized that I was blacking out and that I would probably die, I yelled "Mike!" to my next younger brother.

Just before I blacked out, I heard Mike yell, "I'm coming, Jim!" He came in from behind and broke a dining room chair over Dad's head and shoulders. Apparently, he had been watching from behind the couch in the living room. Dad went down, just like in the old Western saloon fights, with one exception, the chair wasn't a movie prop, it was real. Those were the days when "Maverick" was a big hit TV show. Brothers Bret and Bart Maverick would often refer to one another as "Brother Bret" or "Brother Bart." So, when I came to, I said to Mike in fine Maverick form, "Thank you, Brother Mike," and he said, "You're welcome, Brother Jim." Then, I went to bed to catch a couple hours sleep before I ran my paper routes and went to school. I resolved to learn how to fight, and I did.

"Get up, Clark!"

Bad Dad

When I was twelve, I made another attempt at assuming the position as "head of household." I had been on the streets long enough to learn a thing or two about hand-to-hand combat. My first lesson was when "Smith" from across the street trained me to take over his early paper route. We were at the paper office at three in the morning and he was rolling the papers. I offered to help, and he told me to keep my mouth shut until he told me to open it. So, I curled up on one of the steel tables to nap until it was time to go. It was cold outside, very cold.

The temperature was zero and the wind chill factor was about ten below. Not good, but it was a living. I don't know how long I was asleep. All I know is that Smith woke me up by throwing a three-pound morning newspaper at me as he yelled, "Get up, Clark!" It was Thursday, and the grocery coupons were out, so it was the biggest edition of the week. The paper hit me square in the privates. If you've never been hit in the privates with a three-pound projectile traveling at the speed of light, no amount of description will adequately explain how it feels; especially if you're curled up on a steel table when it happens, and when you reach for your privates (to see if there is any hope of a future family) you fall off the table and land hard on a concrete floor three feet below. Not good.

When I hit the floor, my head hit first, and I was knocked out cold. Smith's answer to that delay in his daily schedule was to pour a six-ounce syrupy Coke over my face to wake me up. The Coke went all over my face, neck, and head, and down into my sweatshirt; then, when we finally got on our bikes and ran the route, it froze. Not good, but tolerable. "Get up, Clark, it's time to go," is all Smith said.

Apparently, landing on a concrete street is about the same as landing on a concrete floor.

Bad Dad

As we ran the route, my privates were swollen like grapefruits, and it hurt like you wouldn't believe to peddle the bike. I don't want to get sidetracked on privates, but they don't respond well to early morning attacks. The Coke was frozen around my head, neck, and chest, and my fingers were about to freeze off (no gloves yet, hadn't received my first check).

It occurred to me that a two-week training period with Smith would be a long haul. So, I did what I felt was necessary. As we rode the route throwing papers, I kept my eyes open for a remedy, an equalizer, if you will. I finally found it, a two by four. There it was, just lying there on the street by the curb as if Fate had left it there for Little Jimmy. So, I hit Smith across the back of the head with it and knocked him off his bicycle. He went down hard, on the concrete street. Apparently, landing on a concrete street is about the same as landing on a concrete floor; Smith was out cold. So, I took the second Coke that he had been drinking (it was in his paper bag), and I poured it over his head; I saved a few sips for myself. The Coke went all over his face, neck, and head, and down into his sweatshirt; then, it froze. That woke him up. "Get up, Smith, we have a route to run." I had no more problems with Smith.

Having done well in the Welterweights with Smith, I decided that I was ready for Round Two with Dad in what I considered the Heavy Weights. It was a big move up. Dad was bigger than Smith, and he carried weapons of what I viewed were potentially WMDs; that is, Weapons of My Destruction; big glass ashtrays, full, longneck beer bottles, little, short (easy to conceal) paring knives, big butcher knives, and belts.

Little short paring knives (SPKs) and big butcher knives (BBKs) are personal carry weapons.

Bad Dad

Big glass ashtrays (BGAs) and full, long neck beer bottles (LNBs) are airborne weapons. Fortunately, they make a very different and distinct sound as they fly through the air. A big glass ashtray flies fast, like a flying saucer, and it has a quiet whistling sound, while a full, longneck beer bottle flies more slowly, and has a loud loping sound like a Viet Nam era Huey helicopter. The key to surviving these attacks is to recognize them instantly, so you know how much time you have to take cover and respond.

It's also important to instantly remember that the assault may be a double assault; that is, a saucer immediately followed by a Huey, or a Huey immediately followed by a saucer. If it's a double assault, it's better if the saucer comes first, because if the Huey comes first the sound is so loud that it almost drowns out the sound of the saucer. I learned that the hard way, it was too close for comfort. I ducked just in time as a BGA buried itself two inches deep into the plaster wall right behind my head.

Little short paring knives (SPKs) and big butcher knives (BBKs) are personal carry weapons; that is, the attacker holds them as he delivers his assault. They're easier to deal with than saucers and Hueys because the attacker can't physically move across the room to attack you as quickly as the saucer or Huey can fly through the air to hit you. If you're alert, you can see the attack coming; the key is to stay alert.

The butcher knife fight isn't close up, whereas a paring knife fight is. A butcher knife is a more honest weapon, you can see it as the attacker comes at you, whereas with a paring knife, you can't. The attacker typically keeps it hidden until he's close enough to stick you.

A belt doesn't sound like a very dangerous weapon,
andit isn't unless it wakes you up during the
night across your eyes.

Bad Dad

Then, by the time you know he has it, it's too late. It only takes one well-placed stick, to the kidneys for example, and it's game over; adios Little Jimmy.

So, early on I developed the habit of always assuming Dad was double carry; that is, if the butcher knife didn't work, he had a paring knife in reserve for a secondary sneak attack to be immediately executed after.

I had disarmed him from the butcher knife. That policy served me well on more than one occasion. Man, I hate paring knives. A belt doesn't sound like a very dangerous weapon, and it isn't unless it wakes you up during the night across your eyes. Never good. After one of our knock down drag out evenings at home, sweet home, Dad decided to teach me a lesson in respect. So, he came upstairs into my room where I was asleep in the top bunk.

I was asleep in the top bunk because brother Mike thought it was funny to pee the bed and let it drip through on brother Jim. He was eleven years old, he didn't have to pee the bed. But, that was his "excuse" for peeing on brother Jim, and Mom believed Little Mikey when he told her it was an accident (she didn't see him grinning as she left the room). We both knew better, but Mom didn't. So, when she wasn't looking, I "helped" Little Mikey move to the lower bunk. We told Mom that Little Mikey had decided that he liked the lower bunk better; problem solved, everyone happy, and dry.

Back to Belt man. If you've never been hit hard across the eyes with a belt while you were asleep, no amount of description will adequately explain how it feels; it hurts and it burns like fire. It feels like someone has just thrown liquid fire or acid in your face.

I did what any self-respecting blind drummer would do; I crawled over under my drum set and took cover.

Bad Dad

Your eyes immediately swell shut in a protective mode. Your natural reaction is to jump up and take cover; but, that isn't so easy if you're asleep in the top bunk when the attack comes. I fell hard four or five feet to the floor, and then I realized two things; first, I was blind, and second, the attack wasn't over. Dad just kept thrashing away with the belt across my head, neck, and shoulders. Each hit hurt and burned like the first. So I did what any self-respecting blind drummer would do; I crawled over under my drum set and took cover. That gave me some relief, and a chance to formulate a plan for a counterattack. Dad just kept coming. He kept slamming the belt into the drum set and cymbals, but he couldn't reach me. He just kept yelling, "How do you like that, you little son-of-a-b----!? Huh!? What are you going to do about that, you little bas-
---!?"

Side note: "Son-of-a-B----", "Little Bas----", and "Pimply-Faced Little Bas----" were Dad's nicknames for me; sometimes "Big Smoke." Of the four, I preferred Big Smoke; I thought it had an aristocratic sound. Once, when the lady at the bank asked me for childhood nickname, I slipped and said, "Little Bas----". She said, "Oh, my." Oh my, was right. I couldn't have said it better.

When Dad asked me, "What are you going to do about that, you little bas----?", I told him.

"Just as soon as I can see (my vision was beginning to return), I'm going to kick your a--- good."

He just kept thrashing away and said, "Oh, is that right, you little son-of-a-b----!? Well, come on out of there and try it!" So, when I could see again, I did.

It was cold outside, real cold, and my eyes hurt.

Bad Dad

After it was over, Mom told me I shouldn't hit my father, and my brothers told me I shouldn't hit Dad. I told them I knew that they were right, that I shouldn't hit Dad, and I told them I didn't like hitting Dad. But, Dad shouldn't try to blind me in my sleep. Then, I told Dad that my room was off limits and that if he ever came into my room again without permission, he would get more of the same, except worse. He never came into my room again; so, I had a relatively safe place to sleep. I caught a couple of hours sleep, ran my routes, and went to school. It was cold outside, real cold, and my eyes hurt.

The physical violence on Mom was bad; it was very bad. As I've said, at one point Dad punched her in the face so hard that her false teeth came through her lower lip. The language he used on her was bad, too. I mean filthy. Every filthy, vile thing that a man could say to a woman he said to her, in front of her boys. That's all I'll say, it was just too filthy to repeat here. The more I heard, and the more I saw, the more fed up I got. I loved my mom, and things got to where I just felt like I couldn't let her be treated that way anymore. The hard part was, I loved my dad too, and I didn't want to do what I knew down deep would have to be done to fix things. But, right is right, and wrong is wrong, and I felt it was my first responsibility to protect my mom and brothers. So, I did.

As are most alcoholics, Dad was a bully. Just like schoolyard bullies (like my paper route mentor Smith), bullies only understand one thing, brute force. They'll do to you whatever they think they can get away with, and most of the time the only way to stop them is with physical encouragement. And, so it was with Dad.

The table exploded into a thousand pieces
and the chairs went flying.

Bad Dad

We lived in a shotgun house; that is, when you walked into the front door you were immediately in the front room; then, the front room poured into the dining room; then, the dining room poured into the kitchen. You could literally stand in the front room and shoot a shotgun through the house without hitting any walls; hence, the moniker "shotgun house'.

On Saturday mornings, Dad used to like to sit at the dining room table, with his back to the kitchen facing the front door and drink. As the day wore on, he would get drunker and drunker. Then, the foul language would start, and then the violence. One Saturday, I came into the house through the kitchen, and I decided that it was time for Round Two. In essence, I decided that it was time to become Head of Household and calm things down. So I stopped at the dining room table and told Dad that I had made a decision. He had just started drinking, so he was a long way from drunk. Nonetheless, he said, "Oh you did, did you? What did you decide, Big Smoke?"

I said, "I've decided that you aren't going to beat on Mom anymore."

Then, he jumped up and said, "What the h--- are you going to do about it?" So, I hit him. It was a good one, a solid right powerhouse to the jaw. He didn't go down, he went flying. He landed in the next room, at the other end of the kitchen, and hit Mom's kitchen table. The table exploded into a thousand pieces and the chairs went flying. When I went out to check on him, he was lying in a pile of kindling wood that used to be the table, and he was out cold. Then, Mikey came in.

You've killed Dad!" "You've killed Dad!"

Bad Dad

When he saw Dad lying there on the floor out cold, he started yelling at the top of his lungs, "Jim's killed Dad!" "Jim's killed Dad!" The summer windows were open, and all of the neighbors for ten miles or so could hear every word; always nice to have the Clarks as neighbors. That's when my other brothers Carl and Bill, and Mom came running.

Mom took one look at Dad and started yelling, "You've killed your father!"

Then, my other brothers joined in, "You've killed Dad!" "You've killed Dad!" What a nightmare. I told all of them that Dad wasn't dead. I told them to throw some water on him and he would come to. Then I left to collect my paper routes.

When I heard the sirens and saw the ambulance heading for my house, I thought I had better go home and see how things were going. Dad didn't look dead, but who knows? You haven't lived until you must follow the ambulance home to see if you really did kill your dad. I had a lot of thoughts going through my head, like whether I should run and just keep running, or take my lumps, do my time, and hope for an early parole. Really, that's what was going through my head as I followed the ambulance home. When I got there, the ambulance was just leaving on its way to the hospital. There were Mom and the brothers four looking at me like I was Hannibal Lecter. Mom told me I shouldn't hit my father, and the brothers four told me I shouldn't hit Dad.

My grandmother reminded me that the Bible says to honor thy father and thy mother. They were right, but Dad shouldn't beat on Mom.

The new table exploded into a thousand pieces and the chairs went flying.

Bad Dad

Dad just had a bruised jaw (not broken, just a hairline crack), a couple of cracked ribs, a couple of black eyes (he looked like a raccoon for a month), and some swelling. He didn't even have to stay overnight at the hospital, they just wrapped his ribs and sent him home. He never hit Mom again.

After a couple of months, when his ribs were healed, Dad started in again with the filthy language against Mom. I figured that the language was a step backward towards more physical violence; so, the next Saturday morning I stopped by the dining room table again. The conversation was almost identical to the first one. I made my little announcement that I had made another decision, to which he replied, "Oh you did, did you? What did you decide, Big Smoke?"

I said, "I've decided that you aren't going to cuss Mom out anymore."

Then, he jumped up and said, "What the h--- are you going to do about it?" Either Dad was a slow learner, or he had a bad memory. Whatever, I hit him, again. It was another good one, a solid right powerhouse to the jaw. He didn't go down, he went flying, again. He landed in the next room, at the other end of the kitchen, and hit the new kitchen table that Mom had just bought, the one that replaced the one into which he had crashed after the first announcement. Apparently, table are tables. The new table exploded into a thousand pieces and the chairs went flying. When I went out to check on him, he was lying in a pile of kindling wood that used to be the table, and he was out cold.

Two decisions announced, two knockouts, and two missions accomplished. Dad never hit Mom again, and he stopped using filthy language on her.

Bad Dad

Then, Mikey came in. When he saw Dad lying there on the floor out cold, he yelled at the top of his lungs, "Jim's killed Dad!" "Jim's killed Dad!" The summer windows were still open, and the neighbors for ten miles could hear every word; again, sure glad the Clarks haven't moved. That's when my other brothers Carl and Bill, and Mom came running.

Mom took one look at Dad and yelled, "You've killed your father!"

Then, my other brothers joined in, "You've killed Dad!" "You've killed Dad!" What a nightmare. I told them all that Dad wasn't dead. I told them to throw some water on him and he would come to. Then, I left to collect my paper routes.

When it was all over, it turned out to be the same scenario as the first time. The ambulance came, the ambulance left, Mom told me I shouldn't hit my father, the brothers four told me I shouldn't hit Dad, and grandmother reminded me that the Bible says to honor thy father and thy mother. They were right; but, Dad shouldn't beat on Mom, or use filthy language on her. Two decisions announced, two knockouts, and two missions accomplished. Dad never hit Mom again, and he stopped using filthy language on her. That was when Mom decided that she hated me for beating on her husband; she hated me from that day on until the day she died.

It would be easy to get the idea that Mom was a cold-hearted, hateful person. She wasn't. Nothing could be further from the truth.

All Mom ever wanted was what all little girls want...

Bad Dad

I never met a person with a better heart, I never met a woman who worked harder to make a good home for her family, and I met no one who would do more for a stranger. Mom saw nothing but the good in people, she just seemed to not see the bad. Her constant admonition was: "If you don't have something good to say about someone, don't say anything at all."

Mom was raised in an environment that made the environment in which I was raised look like a Sunday afternoon picnic; especially when you consider that she was a girl. Her father was a drunk, a mean drunk. She told me the story of one cold, dark winter night when she and her mother ran across a snow-covered field in their nightgowns trying to escape her father. He was chasing them with a shotgun intending to kill them. A six-year-old little girl running for her life, in a cold winter night, across a frozen snow-covered field, trying to escape the one person on whom she should have been able to depend to protect her, her father.

All Mom ever wanted was what all little girls want; to be safe, and to be loved by her protector (father/husband). She just never got it. When I looked at Mom, I saw a little girl in a big girl's body; Little Betty Ann on the inside, all Grown Up Betty on the outside. Mom did the best she could do, with what she knew, and with what she had. Isn't that pretty much what we all do? No one is hurting Mom now; she's with her real Protector, she's with Jesus.

After each knock down drag out fight, Dad would go out to my Aunt Reba and Uncle Wendell's house (grandmother lived with them) and tell them that Little Jimmy had beat him up again; he would show them his bruises to get sympathy.

More than one clown got a little tune up from
Little Jimmy. Dad may have been a drunk,
but he was still MY dad.

Bad Dad

He just didn't think to tell them WHY I had hit him. I could tell by the way they treated me this was going on, so one day I stood in a phone booth in the subzero cold and called my uncle to tell him the whole story. He didn't believe me, he just listened and then hung up without saying a word. That hurt almost as bad as a belt in the eyes.

In a small town like the one in which I was raised, police runs for domestic disturbance and ambulance runs are reported in the paper, on the front page. That made for some interesting remarks at school. "Hey, Clark! I saw your Dad in the paper again..." More than one clown got a little tune up from Little Jimmy. Dad may have been a drunk, but he was still MY dad.

It isn't easy mounting a coup and becoming Head of Household at age twelve, and there is a lot of collateral damage. In any house, there can be only one Head of Household, just as in any kingdom, there can be only one King. Unfortunately, in the Clark Kingdom, the price I paid for keeping peace in the teepee was high. Mom hated me for beating on her husband, and the brothers four hated me for telling them what to do. My grandmother still loved me, but she sat me down one day and explained that Dad was her son, and how much it hurt her to see what was going on. That almost killed me. Little Jimmy loved Grandma with all of his heart, and the thought that he was doing something that hurt Grandma really hurt. But, Dad shouldn't beat on Mom, or use filthy language on her.

Hated is not too strong of a word. To this day, some 50 years later, the brothers four don't speak.

What the brothers four don't seem to recognize is...

Bad Dad

All I've ever heard was, "You weren't our Dad, you didn't have any right to tell us what to do." They're right. I wasn't their Dad, and I had no right to tell them what to do.

What the brothers four don't seem to recognize is that if I hadn't done what I did, some of them, or Mom, might have been killed. Brother Jeff tells the story of waking up one night just in time to roll out of bed as Dad plunged a butcher knife into the mattress on which he was sleeping. As he tells it, a split second later and it would have been over. Unknown to Mom or the brothers four are the times I intervened just in time, like the time I walked into the kitchen to find Dad behind Mom getting ready to cave her skull in with a full, long neck beer bottle. The brothers four don't know about the understanding that the police chief and I had.

After one of the knock-down drag-out drunken battles at 310 (our address when I was a child), the Chief of Police took me aside and out into the yard and told me what he planned to do. He said that if things kept going the way that they were, he was going to "take you boys out of there." I asked him if we, the brothers, would be allowed to stay together. He said probably not, that no one wanted to adopt five boys. So, I "cut a deal" with him. I asked him to hold off until I told him that things were so bad that I couldn't handle it. He agreed. It was two in the morning, and I had to get up in an hour to run my routes and go to school; so, I thanked the Chief and went back into the house and went to bed.

The brothers four don't know how often Satan or one of his demons whispered in my ear and told me to just kill Dad and put him out of our misery. Not once, not twice, but often.

No one beats on my Mom, or my brothers, without paying the price; no one, not even Dad.

Bad Dad

If I hadn't accepted Jesus as my Savior when I was eleven, I would have done it, no question about it. The Holy Spirit of God whispering in my other ear was all that stopped me. Praise God Jehovah of the Bible for Sunday School, for church camp, for Jesus, and for the Holy Spirit.

The brothers four don't know what I did after each knock-down drag-out fight during which I had to hit Dad. After it was all over, I went outside where I could be alone, and I cried my eyes out. I remember like it was yesterday, standing outside at two o'clock in the morning, in the cold dark night, in the snow, in sub-zero weather, crying. I felt guilty for hitting my dad, and I felt ALONE, very alone. I loved Dad, and it hurt my heart to do what I had to do to get things under control. I loved Mom, and it hurt my heart for her to hate me for hitting her husband. I loved my brothers, and it hurt my heart they hated me for telling them what to do. It just hurt. So, after a big battle, I would go outside and cry it out, and then go on about my business. No one beats on my Mom, or my brothers, without paying the price; no one, not even Dad.

After the first few times, I stopped crying.

The brothers four don't know about the healing process. Dad's cracked ribs healed, and his black eyes and bruises went away. My heart will never heal and it will never stop hurting. Praise God for the Holy Spirit, my Comforter, who makes the pain that comes with memories bearable.

NO MAN was ever prouder of his brothers than I am of mine. All four are good men, and I'm proud to be their brother. I would lay down my life for any of them, in a heartbeat. And yet, we have NO fellowship, they haven't spoken for years. This is a prime example of how good Satan is at his job. He tears down and he destroys.

The violence was under control...

Bad Dad

Here, he has destroyed the blessing of family. Other than one's salvation, there are few greater losses that one can suffer.

Mom and the brothers four were right. I shouldn't have hit Mom's husband, my dad, and I didn't have the right to tell my brothers what to do. It seemed like the right thing to do at the time: a measured response, I think they call it, and it was effective. The violence was under control, the filthy language ended, and the brothers Clark got to stay together. Not bad work for a twelve-year-old.

Before you decide that Dad was a total low life, a total Bad Dad, let me tell you a little more about him. As you work your way through these few short retellings, you'll see a different side of Dad. You'll see a man who had a good heart, albeit a troubled one. Satan destroys good people too.

"Mom, they need me".

Good Dad

Dad's father was an alcoholic. My grandmother told me a story about the times when my dad was a little boy he would chase his father down the sidewalk, begging him to take him along. She said that my grandfather wouldn't say a word, he would just slam the gate in my dad's little face and walk off. My grandmother said this happened time after time, repeatedly. What does that do to a little boy?

When my dad was 17, he lied about his age and joined the Navy. It was the middle of WWII, and my dad was very patriotic. He felt compelled to serve his country, even if he had to lie to do it, and even if it meant he might not come home. Dad never talked about his service, but my uncle, who was in the Navy with Dad, told me some things. My dad was a medic. My uncle said that at one point my dad was hanging off the back of a battleship in the Pacific Ocean holding an injured soldier in his arms. He said that my dad was holding the soldier's brains in with his hand because the soldier's skull had been blown away. What does that do to a young man of 17?

At the end of the war, my dad was given an Honorable Discharge. But, when the Korean War broke out, he reenlisted. My grandmother told me it almost killed her. She told him he had served his country once, and she said that she begged him not to go. She said that when she asked my dad why he had reenlisted, all he would say was, "Mom, they need me".

The only story my dad ever told me about either war was about seeing little children starving to death with their little stomachs bloated.

My dad was honest. "Tell the TRUTH, ----! There's nothing worse than a ---- liar!"

Good Dad

He said that they would jump into the ocean and try to swim out to the ship as it pulled away from the docks hoping to eat the garbage that the cooks threw over the side. He only told me that once, and that's all he ever told me. He was half-popped when he told me; he just let out a profanity and took another drink as his eyes welled with tears.

My mother told me that before Korea my dad loved life. She said he saw the beauty in everything and in everyone, but when he came back from Korea, he was a different person.

My dad was patriotic, his record shows that. I grew up in a very patriotic household (between knock-down drag-out battles). My mother ran the Jehovah's Witnesses off the porch with a broom, because they wouldn't salute the flag, while my dad screamed profanities at them for all the neighbors to hear as they scrambled for safety. Most neighbors nodded approval to Mr. Clark, the veteran, and to Mrs. Clark, the broom-master.

My dad was honest. "Tell the TRUTH, ----! There's nothing worse than a ---- liar!" If I heard that once growing up, I heard it a million times.

My dad took pride in his work. My uncle told me that Dad had a reputation at General Motors for being the best that General Motors had in skilled trades (my uncle was in management at GM). He said Dad could mill a helicopter turbine engine rotor within a millionth of an inch. I also had a client who knew Dad from work who told me the same thing. "Be the BEST, ----!" If I heard that once growing up, I heard it a million times.

"What the h--- do you want?"

Good Dad

My dad wanted more for his boys than he had. "Get an education! Use your head, not your back! Don't work in a ---- factory!" If I heard that once growing up, I heard it a million times.

One time when I was eleven, I went into my dad's room and I asked him if he had a minute. He said, "What the h--- do you want?" I told him that the tee shirt I had on was the only shirt I had, and I pointed at the shoulder as I told him it had a hole in it. He said, "What the h--- are you telling me for?" So, I left the room. As I stood in the hallway, I was thinking about the "Leave It to Beaver" television programs I had been watching. Beaver had told his dad Ward that he needed something and the entire family jumped into the family station wagon and headed to the mall. It was then that I realized that we Clarks were not a Leave It to Beaver type family. So, I went back into Dad's room again, and I asked him if he had a minute. He said, "What the h--- do you want now?" I asked him if I could get a job. He said, "Get the h--- out of here, I don't care what you do." So, I left his room and headed out the front door in search of employment. As I went past Mom, she asked me where I was going. When I told her that her eleven-year-old Little Jimmy was finally going out into the world looking for a job, she exploded. I told her that Dad had given me permission, so she needed to talk to him. In my mind, "Get the h--- out of here, I don't care what you do" meant, "Yes son, you may get a job." As Mom headed for Dad's room, I headed for town.

One afternoon I came into the house while Dad was sitting on his ex-throne at the dining room table. As I lumbered through, he said, "Where have you been?"

"You ain't The Billy Graham just because
you've been to youth group."

Good Dad

When I told him I had been at youth group, at church, he said, "You ain't The Billy Graham just because you've been to youth group." To be honest, it had never occurred to me that I might be "The Billy Graham", just because I went to youth group. That struck me as the funniest thing that I'd ever heard. Now, a half-century later, I still laugh every time I think of it. Hmmm. "The Billy Graham."

Okay, so what was it with my dad? What was his problem? I'll tell you what it was with my dad, it's very simple. He was a man who knew Jesus as his Savior, but let Satan steal his joy, ruin his testimony, and destroy his life. It isn't any harder than that.

Look at my dad's life, and what do you see?

I see a little boy who wanted what every little boy wants, a daddy who would love him and spend time with him. Did he have it? No, Satan made sure that he didn't. My grandfather, Dad's father, was an alcoholic too. He never gave my Dad the time of day.

I see a young man who loved his country so much he would lie about his age just to have a chance to risk his life for it; a young man who held a fellow patriot in his arms while he held the man's brains in until the man finally took his last breath. "Mom, they need me." What kind of a young man is that?

I see a man who was honest; a man who yelled, and yelled, and yelled (counseled his boys), to "Tell the TRUTH, ----! There's nothing worse than a ---- liar!" What kind of man cares enough to teach his boys to be honest men?

I was there when Dad and Mom accepted
Jesus as their Savior.

Good Dad

I see a man who was proud of his work but wanted more for his boys. "Be the BEST, ----!" "Get an education! Use your head, not your back! Don't work in a ---- factory!" What kind of man wants a better life for his boys than he had?

I see a man who wanted to teach his boys self-reliance. "What the h--- are you telling me for?" means, "If you need a tee shirt, get a job and earn a tee shirt." What kind of man tries to teach his boys to be self-reliant men?

I could go on and on, back and forth, back and forth, but the bottom line is the same. My dad was either a worthless drunk who couldn't care less about anyone other than himself, or he was a good man who simply gave up the fight and let Satan win. I think it was the latter, and I'll tell you why.

I was there when Dad and Mom accepted Jesus as their Savior. I was little, but I was there. We went to a little church at the end of the street. I don't remember the details, but I remember how things changed. Dad stopped beating on Mom and cussing her out, and Mom started singing while she stood at the sink and washed the dishes. She used to sing "In the Garden": "I walk through the garden alone, while the dew is still on the roses, and the Voice I hear, as we tarry there..." That's all I remember, but I remember how happy she was. Things were good for a while, then they changed.

Worthless drunks who couldn't care less about anyone other than themselves don't take their family to church, not even for a little while.

The elder was a good man, or he wouldn't have
been serving as an elder...

Good Dad

Dad worked part-time for one of the elders in the church who owned a truck dealership. One Saturday morning the dealership took delivery of a new truck. When the elder's wife (she worked there too) saw the engine, she told her husband, "Bill, this isn't a new truck, look at the grease on the engine."

The elder took one look, picked up a hose, and said, "It is now," as he sprayed the grease off with a hose. Dad saw what happened, and that was that; he quit.

"Tell the TRUTH, ----! There's nothing worse than a ---- liar!" I don't remember whether that's when he stopped going to church, but I do know that it blew him out of the water. The elder was his mentor and example in Jesus.

Regardless of what our elders do or don't do, each of us are responsible for our personal walk with God. But, this is a good example of how Satan operates. He'll use anything to tear down and destroy; anything, anytime, anyone. This was a good one, a three for one, you might say. The elder's testimony was destroyed, Dad's joy was diminished when he lost the leadership of his mentor, and the elder's wife's joy was diminished when she saw her husband, her spiritual leader, do what he did.

Dad didn't become a soul winner for Jesus like he might have. How many are in Hell today because of this one incident, because the elder dropped his guard for just a split second? That's all Satan needs, just a split second: one little whisper in the ear, "Just spray it off" is all it takes. The elder was a good man, or he wouldn't have been serving as an elder; he just let Satan catch him off guard with a sucker punch.

Dad went to rehab over 20 times...

Good Dad

Worthless drunks who couldn't care less about anyone other than themselves don't quit their jobs when they see something dishonest happen; they don't care.

When Dad worked at General Motors, they had one of the best health care plans in the world. It was a good thing for Dad they did, considering he had five boys. One benefit afforded by his plan was rehab from alcohol.

An employee with a drinking problem (Dad qualified) could go to a rehab center for up to several weeks at a time to get treatment, to dry out. Over the 30 some years he worked at GM, Dad went to rehab over 20 times for a week or two each time. Every time he would come home it was the same. Things would go great for a while, Mom would be happy for a while, and then, kaboom! It would start all over again. All it took was one little whisper in the ear, "Just one drink won't hurt."

Worthless drunks who couldn't care less about anyone other than themselves don't go to rehab over 20 times; they just don't bother.

When Dad died, my brothers made the funeral arrangements for funeral number one, and I made the funeral arrangements for funeral number two. Maybe in the sequel to this book, if there is a sequel to this book, I'll explain why we had to have two funerals; one for just my dad's sister, Aunt Reba, and one for everyone else, the one to which Mom went (hint). I doubt there will be a sequel, but who knows? Maybe when I get old, I'll want to talk about the past.

The funeral I arranged was just a small memorial service.

The brothers four hired a long-haired hippy preacher
who played a guitar before he spoke.

Good Dad

I asked a friend who was a kindly, old-fashioned, old-time-religion gentleman pastor, to say a few words of encouragement for the benefit of my aunt. My wife and I, and Aunt Reba and Uncle Wendell, were the only ones there, other than the pastor and the ladies from his church who he brought to sing. The pastor had never met my dad, so before he came he called me and asked me about Dad's life. He really took some time, as if he was really interested. The pastor knew about my Dad's struggles with alcohol, but he just forgot to mention them. He talked about my dad's military service, his career at General Motors, and his love for his wife and five boys. The memorial he gave was the most beautiful memorial service I had ever heard, or have heard since. It did what needed to be done for Aunt Reba; she never quit telling Little Jimmy how beautiful "her Jimmy's" service was (Dad and I have the same name, so he was called Jimmy and I was called Little Jimmy). After the pastor spoke, the ladies sang the old-fashioned church hymns that Dad liked, while the organist played.

The funeral that my brothers arranged was different. To begin with, the brothers four hired a long-haired hippy preacher who played a guitar before he spoke. Let me just say that again, and then drop it; the brothers four hired a long-haired hippy preacher who played a guitar before he spoke. Dad was a WWII/Korean War vet, he wasn't into long-haired hippy types; I don't think he even knew there was such a thing as a long-haired hippy type preacher. I still can't figure how he came to tell this one his life's story; just lonely, I guess.

The message given was different too. The "preacher" told those in attendance that Dad had asked him over just before he died.

With my wife gripping my arm so hard with both hands I couldn't get up...

Good Dad

He said that Dad had told him he felt he had wasted his life on alcohol, and that he was ashamed of his life. Not one good word about Dad's military service, his career at General Motors, his family, or anything else; just that Dad was an old drunk who knew that he had wasted his life. I have very few regrets in my life, but how I handled that situation IS one of them. With my wife gripping my arm so hard with both hands I couldn't get up without making a scene (she wouldn't let go), I maintained my composure, kept my mouth shut, and let him finish his little speech.

If I had it to do over, I would do things differently. I would interrupt the preacher during his speech, help him find a seat in the audience, and then I would tell the crowd about my real dad, the Good Dad. Or I would walk up to the podium and give the preacher one of those solid right powerhouse shots to the jaw that I gave Dad for beating on Mom, and then I would tell the crowd about my real dad, the Good Dad. To this day I can't decide which course of action would have been more appropriate. I guess it's a good thing my wife wouldn't let go of my arm.

Worthless drunks who couldn't care less about anyone other than themselves don't weep bitterly as they tell their pastor they are ashamed of their life because they wasted it on alcohol.

I'm not defending my dad. What he did and how he lived his life was wrong and he knew it. He CHOSE to do what he did; one little temptation, one little decision, at a time. The question is how? How could a man who had such a good heart and who knew Jesus as his Savior, let things get so wrong for so long? Again, the answer is Satan.

Satan hated Dad's guts, and he beat on Dad
every moment of every day...

Good Dad

Satan hated Dad's guts, and he beat on Dad every moment of every day until Dad just finally gave up, defeated. Satan won, he totally and completely destroyed Dad's life and our family with it.

There are only two ways out...

Two Ways Out

There are only two ways out of the hell hole in which you live. You can take the hand of the drug dealer or some other lowlife and follow Satan, or you can take the hand of Jesus and follow God.

If you follow Satan, you'll end up dead or in prison for the rest of your life. Then, when you die, you'll go to Hell and be tortured while you burn in the lake of fire forever.

If you follow God, you'll live a quality life of purpose, a good life. God will be with you every step of the way through good times and bad. Then, when you die, you'll go to Heaven to live with God forever. In Heaven there is no grief, no sorrow, no pain, and no suffering. There is only the joy and peace of being in God's presence as you experience the love and beauty of God.

I KNOW what I'm talking about. I was the boy in this book. I lived in a real-life hell hole. I took Jesus' hand and followed God out. He has been with me every step of the way since. My brother and friend didn't take Jesus' hand. My brother was locked up in boys' school and our friend was locked up in prison.

Read the rest of this book and learn how to escape your hell hole.

Satan hates your guts.

Good and Evil

God is PURE GOOD. There is no evil in Him.

God loves you. He loves you more than words can describe. He wants what's best for you. He wants you to be with Him in Heaven. He has done everything that can be done to make it possible for you to spend eternity with Him, up to and including sending His Son Jesus to die on the Cross to pay for your sins.

Jesus is God's Son. He is EVERYTHING. He is PERFECTION. He is the embodiment of God because His love is total and complete. He is our Savior, He is our Protector, and He is our Example. Without Jesus, we HAVE nothing, we ARE nothing.

Satan is PURE EVIL. There is no good in him.

Satan was an angel in Heaven. He wanted to be God and take His place in Heaven so he started a fight with God. God won. He threw Satan and his buddies out of Heaven. Since then, Satan has been trying to get even with God. He can't whip God, so he tries to hurt God by hurting God's children, you and me.

Get this, if you don't get anything else. Satan hates your guts. He is a dirty, filthy, stinking, disgusting, greasy, EVIL creature who wants to destroy you. He is a vicious animal who will rip you apart and laugh while he's doing it. When you die he wants you to spend the rest of eternity in Hell being tortured in a burning lake of fire. Until you die he wants you to live a miserable life. That's what Satan wants for you.

Hell is real. It is a horrible place of torment and torture. Those who go to Hell burn in a literal lake of fire. Ever burn

And whosoever was not found written in the book of life
was cast into the lake of fire."

your finger on a hot stove? How about burning your whole body like that, with one very big exception. When you burn your finger you know it will stop hurting after a while. When you are in Hell your entire body will burn. It will hurt just like your finger hurt, but it will never stop. You will burn forever while Satan laughs at you and mocks you.

Hell is the automatic, it is the default destination. You don't have to do anything to go to Hell. If you do nothing, you will wake up in Hell when you die and that is where you will suffer for eternity. If you want to go to Heaven when you die, you must DO something. You must be SAVED.

Revelation 20:15

"And whosoever was not found written in the book of life was cast into the lake of fire."

"For all have sinned, and come short of the glory of God."

Saved

The Bible says everyone has sinned, including you. It says the penalty for sinning is death, meaning eternal punishment in Hell.

The Bible says there is nothing you can do to make up for the sins you have done. It says the best thing you ever did was like a dirty rag in God's eyes. He just is not impressed by what man does.

Your sins must be paid for. Someone must pay for your sins. Since you can't do it God sent His son Jesus to do it for you. When Jesus shed his blood on the Cross your sins were paid for with His blood. Your Sin Debt was marked PAID IN FULL. That's why Jesus is called Savior. When He died on the Cross for you, He SAVED you from an eternity of torture and torment in Hell.

Don't think you need a savior because you've lived a good life? Be careful with that. Don't be fooled. That is exactly what the "Father of Lies" Satan wants you to believe. Remember, God is not impressed with man's good deeds. Your living a good life means nothing to Him if you reject the price His Son Jesus paid on the Cross for you.

Romans 3:23-26

"For all have sinned, and come short of the glory of God."

Isaiah 64:6

"But we are all as an unclean thing, and all our righteousnesses are as filthy rags."

"For the wages of sin is death; but the gift of God is eternal life through Jesus Christ our Lord."

Saved

Romans 6:23

"For the wages of sin is death; but the gift of God is eternal life through Jesus Christ our Lord."

"I accept your gift of eternal life through Jesus' shed blood on the Cross. Thank you, God, for your mercy and love."

Steps to Salvation

Steps to Salvation

There are five simple steps to being saved.

1. Recognize and admit that you have sinned.

2. Recognize and admit that there is nothing you can do to pay for your sins, that you need a savior.

3. Recognize and believe that Jesus paid for your sins with His shed blood on the Cross, HE is your Savior.

4. Ask God to forgive you for your sins and accept His gift of eternal life through Jesus' shed blood on the Cross.

5. Thank God and praise Him for His mercy and love.

Bow your head. Bow your head now and pray this simple prayer:

"God, I know I have sinned. I know there is nothing I can do to make up for the sins I have committed. I believe Jesus shed His blood on the Cross to pay for my sins. God, please forgive me for my sins.

I accept your gift of eternal life through Jesus' shed blood on the Cross. Thank you, God, for your mercy and love."

The split second you pray this prayer your sins will be forgiven and God's angels will rejoice and write your name in the Lamb's Book of Life (God's reservation book for Heaven). You will have a NEW BEGINNING. Your Bible will be your instruction manual for how you are to live your new life.

Read your Bible and you'll know what to do and what not

Don't depend on what feels right.

Steps to Salvation

to do. Don't depend on what feels right. The Bible says the ways of a man seem right to him. Don't depend on what someone else, even a preacher, tells you. Read your Bible and listen to God as He speaks to you through His word. Then you'll know how God expects you to live your life.

Proverbs 21:2

"Every way of man is right in his own eyes…"

Are there any exceptions? Yes. REPENTENCE.

License to Sin

Now that you're saved and your name is written in the Lamb's Book of Life you can live any way you want to, right? WRONG. God makes it very clear that He expects you to live a godly life. He has rules and He expects you to follow them. If you don't you will not "inherit the kingdom of God" when you die, you will inherit Hell, the kingdom of Satan.

What about those who say that once a person has accepted Jesus and has been saved it is impossible for him to go to Hell? They need to read their Bibles. "Know ye not that the unrighteous shall not inherit the kingdom of God?" is about as plain as it can be. It doesn't say, "Know ye not that the unrighteous shall not inherit the kingdom of God, UNLESS they have been saved, in which case they can live any way they want to live." Does it? No, it does not. Live a godless life and you will not go to Heaven when you die, you will go straight to Hell. Period.

Are there any exceptions? Yes. REPENTENCE. If you get on the wrong track after you are saved and you repent, God is faithful to forgive. How many times can you commit the same sins and be forgiven? That's between you and God. Personally, I wouldn't push it.

Just because you receive a gift, that does not mean you have to keep it. You can always give it back.

The same goes for eternal salvation. Just because you accept God's gift of eternal life through Jesus' shed blood on the Cross, that does not mean you have to keep it. All you have to do to give it back is turn your back on God and live a godless life. God doesn't force anyone to join Him in Heaven, God doesn't beg anyone to join Him in Heaven, nor does God let those who live a godless life live with

"If we confess our sins, He is faithful and just to forgive us our sins, and to cleanse us from all unrighteousness."

Him in Heaven. That would defeat the purpose of Heaven, wouldn't it?

1 John 1:9

"If we confess our sins, He is faithful and just to forgive us our sins, and to cleanse us from all unrighteousness."

1 Corinthians 6:9 and 6:10.

"Know ye not that the unrighteous shall not inherit the kingdom of God? Be not deceived: neither fornicators, nor idolaters, nor adulterers, nor effeminate, nor abusers of themselves with mankind, (10) Nor thieves, nor covetous, nor drunkards, nor revilers, nor extortioners, shall inherit the kingdom of God."

Galatians 5:19

"Now the works of the flesh are manifest, which are these: adultery, fornication, uncleanness, lasciviousness, idolatry, witchcraft, hatred, variance, emulations, wrath, strife, seditions, heresies, envyings, murders, drunkenness, revellings, and such like: of the which I tell you before, as I have also told you in time past, that they which do such things shall not inherit the kingdom of God."

Satan has a three-fold plan to destroy you.

A Better Life Now

WHERE is Satan now? Is he in Hell? No, he is not. He is down here on the ground with us.

One day God asked Satan where he had been. Satan answered and told God that he "had been going to and fro in the earth, and from walking up and down in it". Satan was NOT walking to and fro in the earth looking for an ice cream cone. He was walking to and fro in the earth looking for YOU, so he could destroy your life.

Satan has a three-fold plan to destroy you.

First, he wants to steal your soul. He wants to keep you so busy that you don't get around to dealing with where you will spend eternity. He knows that if he can do that long enough, you will wake up one day and find yourself in Hell, forever.

Second, if he can't steal your soul because you get saved, he wants to steal your testimony. He wants to make your life so miserable that no one else will want to get saved to have what you have. WHO wants to get saved and have a miserable life like you? If Satan can't steal your soul he wants to steal your ability to demonstrate what a wonderful and peaceful life a person can have in Jesus.

Third, he wants to steal your joy. There is joy in being saved. There is the peace that only comes from knowing Jesus as your Savior. After sinning with Bathsheba, King David prayed for forgiveness and asked God to "restore unto me the joy of thy salvation". Remember, Satan hates your guts. He does NOT want you to be happy. He does not want you to have peace in your heart and mind. He wants you to be miserable, hopefully so miserable that you even commit suicide. THAT is how much Satan hates you. Believe it.

Thankfully for you and me, God has a plan too.

Satan roams the earth tearing down and destroying lives. He is good at what he does. If you aren't saved you are ON YOUR OWN, and you will lose the attacks Satan levels at you. You are just not up to it. You are just not powerful enough to fight Satan on your own and win. No one is. If you try to do battle with Satan alone, you will lose. Period. Your life will be destroyed and you will end up in Hell when you die.

Thankfully for you and me, God has a plan too. The split second you accept Jesus as your Savior, God will send His Holy Spirit to live in your heart. The Holy Spirit is a real person. His job is to guide you and protect you while you are still on this earth. He is with you every second of every day and He is on guard.

When Satan whispers in your ear and tells you to do something ungodly. the Holy Spirit will whisper in your other ear and suggest that you don't do what Satan is suggesting. He will SUGGEST that you don't do what Satan is suggesting. You have free will, you will make the decision.

When Satan creates circumstances in your life that make you sad, or nervous, or afraid, the Holy Spirit will whisper in your ear a Bible verse that will remind you that God is with you. For example, when you are worried about something the Holy Spirit will whisper "For God hath not given us the spirit of fear, but of power, and of love, and of a sound mind. That will remind you that the fear and worry that you are experiencing is from Satan, not God. Then the Holy Spirit will whisper "And the peace of God, which passeth all understanding, shall keep your hearts and minds through Christ Jesus." That will remind you to say a little prayer and ask God for His peace in your heart. The SPLIT SECOND you ask, God will fill your heart with

What a wonderful blessing from God is His Holy Spirit.
Thank you, Lord.

A Better Life Now

so much joy you will feel like you are going to explode from happiness. The tears will run down your cheeks and you will raise God for His love. That is when Satan will move on to someone else because he will know that he has lost that attack on you. You must be wise enough not to get cocky. Satan will come back, but when he does he'll find the Holy Spirit is still with you. Praise God.

Read your Bible and memorize verses. Then, the Holy Spirit will remind you of the verse you need when you need it. What a wonderful blessing from God is His Holy Spirit. Thank you, Lord.

Job 1:7

"And the LORD said unto Satan, Whence comest thou? Then Satan answered the LORD, and said, From going to and fro in the earth, and from walking up and down in it."

Philippians 4:7

"And the peace of God, which passeth all understanding, shall keep your hearts and minds through Christ Jesus."

2 Timothy 1:7

"For God hath not given us the spirit of fear; but of power, and of love, and of a sound mind."

Psalms 51:12

"Restore unto me the joy of thy salvation; and uphold me with thy free spirit."

Don't ignore Hell. Deal with it. Deal with it NOW.

Epilogue

So now you know the truth. It's up to you to decide where and with whom you will spend eternity.

You can accept God's gift of eternal life through Jesus' shed blood on the Cross and spend eternity with Him in Heaven, or you can do nothing and wake up one day with Satan in Hell. You can live a life before you die that is filled with joy and peace, or you can go through life alone filled with worry, stress, and pain.

It's YOUR decision but remember one thing. Ignoring Hell doesn't make it go away, any more than ignoring a severed arm stops the bleeding. Ignore a severed arm and you'll bleed to death. Ignore Hell and that's where you'll spend eternity.

Don't ignore Hell. Deal with it. Deal with it NOW, before it's too late. Bow your head, repent, and accept God's gift of eternal life through Jesus. Then show God how much you appreciate His gift by living a godly life.

"God, I know I have sinned. I know there is nothing I can do to make up for the sins I have committed. I believe Jesus shed His blood on the Cross to pay for my sins. God, please forgive me for my sins. I accept your gift of eternal life through Jesus' shed blood on the Cross. Thank you, God, for your mercy and love."

Could Satan do the same thing to you?

Epilogue II

Things were rough before I was eleven. Mom told me about the time she decided to leave my dad. I was two years old. She said that she had me in her arms and was heading down the steps in their three-story apartment building when Dad caught her on the landing. He told her that if she didn't stop, he would knock her and me down the steps and kill us both. She said that he had a gallon glass milk bottle in his hands, and he would use it to keep his promise. She said there was no doubt by the look in his eyes that he meant every word of what he had said. So, she went back into the apartment and did as she was told.

Mom hurt nothing by telling me this story; I already knew it, I was there. Any good pediatrician or quantum physicist will tell you that a two-year-old understands what's going on in a situation like that. He doesn't know why, but he knows that Daddy will hurt Mommy and him. His little heart pounds, and it scares him to death, but there's nothing that he can do but cry and hold tight to his mommy.

I tell you this story to illustrate just how far down Satan can grind a man. You don't think that you would ever threaten to kill your wife and son? Look at the picture of my dad when he was young, as he looked at his new baby boy asleep in his cradle. Do you think at that moment that he could have imagined that two short years later he would be threatening to knock him down a flight of stairs and end his life? Do you think that he could have, in his wildest imagination, imagined a life for himself and his family like the one he had; or do you think that he just let his guard down and Satan caught him with one sucker punch too many, and the game was over?

Could Satan do the same thing to you? Could he be working on you right now, one little decision at a time, and

Satan hates your guts, and he'll destroy you in a
heartbeat if you give him half a chance.

Epilogue II

you just haven't noticed? Where will you be two years from now? Satan hates your guts, and he'll destroy you in a heartbeat if you give him half a chance. Don't let your guard down. When it comes to dealing with Satan, you and I aren't special. If we don't cling to Jesus, like Little Jimmy clung to his mommy in the stairwell, it's over; we're done, and we'll be in Hell forever, just where Satan wants us.

Index

A
A Better Life Now 85, 87, 89

B
Bad Dad 15, 17, 19, 21, 23, 25, 27, 29, 31, 33, 35, 37, 39, 41, 43, 45

E
Epilogue 91
Epilogue II 93, 95

G
Good and Evil 69, 71
Good Dad 47, 49, 51, 53, 55, 57, 59, 61, 63, 65

L
License to Sin 81, 83

P
Prologue 13

S
Saved 73, 75
Steps to Salvation 77, 79

T
Two Ways Out 67

Jim Clark is an award-winning internationally-published author. He is the recipient of the International Poetry Society's coveted Editor's Choice Award for his outstanding book of romantic poems:

May I Dream?

A collection of poems on matters of the heart.

Jim Clark Books

Jim Clark's American Library™ is exciting. There are four divisions: Retirement Planning, Romance, Life on Earth, and Textbooks. Regardless of whether you're feeling romantic, planning your retirement, protecting your estate, or preparing for a new career, you'll find the right book in Jim Clark's American Library™.

Jim Clark's books carry a three-fold purpose; to inform, to entertain, and to raise awareness that there are children in America who go to bed hungry.

Jim Clark books are

J. Charles Clark Publishing publications.
All rights reserved, offers limited.

This and other outstanding books by the author may be purchased at:

www.jimclarkbooks.com

To learn how to help feed every hungry child in America visit:

www.jimclarkretirement.com/children

Made in the USA
Monee, IL
25 September 2022

14383045R10057